SMALLVILLE™

ARRIVAL

Superman created by Jerry Siegel
and Joe Shuster

LEVEL 1

SCHOLASTIC

'Arrival' adapted by: Jane Revell
Based on the novelization by Michael Teitelbaum.
Adapted from the teleplay by Alfred Gough and Miles Millar.

Fact Files written by: Jacquie Bloese

Commissioning Editor: Jacquie Bloese

Editor: Jane Rollason

Designer: Dawn Wilson

Picture research: Emma Bree

Photo credits:
Cover and inside images courtesy of Warner Bros.
Page 36: Photodisc/Punchstock.
Page 37: P. Gould/Corbis; Stockbyte/Punchstock.

Mary Glasgow Magazines (Scholastic Ltd.)
Euston House
24 Eversholt Street
London
NW1 1DB

Printed in Singapore. Reprinted in 2007, 2008, 2009, 2010 and 2011.
This edition printed in 2013.

Contents

CLARK KENT

Clark is from another world. He arrives in Smallville in a spaceship. He lives on a farm with his mom and dad, Martha and Jonathan Kent. Clark is very special. He's very strong and he can move very fast.

PLACES

Smallville

A small town in Kansas with a lot of farms.

Smallville High School

Clark and his friends go to school here.

Metropolis

A very big city. It is three hours away from Smallville by train.

LuthorCorp

LuthorCorp have many factories in the USA. They're buying a new one in Smallville. Lionel Luthor works at LuthorCorp in Metropolis.

LANA LANG

Lana lives with her Aunt Nell in a house next to the Kents. Clark loves her but she has a boyfriend.

LEX LUTHOR

Lex is Lionel Luthor's son but he is different from his father. He wants to help people.

PETE ROSS AND CHLOE SULLIVAN

Pete and Chloe are Clark's best friends. Pete is funny and clever but he doesn't like sports. Chloe came to Smallville from Metropolis. She writes for the school newspaper. She likes Clark.

WHITNEY FORDMAN

Whitney is Lana's boyfriend. He's fantastic at sports and is in all the school teams. But he isn't a very nice person.

ARRIVAL

CHAPTER 1
A child arrives

1989, Smallville, Kansas, USA.

Suddenly the sky was dark. There were hundreds of meteors in the sky. They went faster and faster. There was a very small spaceship in the centre of the meteors. There was one person in this spaceship. A child.

■ ■ ■

Nothing happened in Smallville. It was a small town in Kansas and it was a very boring place. Then, one day, everything changed.

Lionel Luthor arrived from Metropolis in his helicopter. He was a rich man, but he was not a nice man. He loved money, not people. His young son Lex sat next to him. Lex was nine years old. He had red hair and blue eyes. His face was white and his eyes were closed. He was very frightened.

'Lex!' shouted his father. 'Open your eyes now!'

'I can't,' Lex said. 'I hate this helicopter.'

'Luthors aren't frightened of anything,' Lionel said. 'Look out of the window – now!'

Lex slowly opened his eyes and looked down.

I'm going to die, he thought.

Two men waited for the helicopter in the car park of an old factory. The men were brothers: Dale and Bill Ross.

'Why does Lionel Luthor want to buy our factory?' asked Dale.

'I don't know,' said Bill, 'but we need his money. He isn't going to change anything. He told us that, and I believe him.'

Jonathan Kent and his wife Martha went into a shop on Main Street. Their faces were brown from the sun and their jeans were old. They lived on a farm.

'Afternoon, Nell,' Jonathan said.

'Hello, Jonathan,' Nell said. She smiled at him. She liked Jonathan.

'Hello, Martha,' she said. She didn't smile at Martha. She didn't like her.

'I'd like some tulips,' said Martha. 'Red tulips, please.'

There was a little girl in the shop. She was very pretty with dark hair. She was three years old.

'Hello, Lana,' said Martha. 'Where are your mom and dad today?'

'They're at the homecoming game*,' Nell said. 'Here are your tulips.' She gave them to Jonathan.

In the street, Martha said sadly, 'Oh Jonathan, I looked at Lana's little face and I ...' She stopped.

'I know, Martha,' said Jonathan. 'We both want a child.'

* High schools in the USA have a big football game every October. It's called the homecoming game. There's a homecoming dance too.

The meteors came closer and closer.

■ ■ ■

At the factory, Lex was bored. He walked away into a cornfield next to the factory.

Lionel Luthor read the papers. 'Where do I put my name?' he asked the Ross brothers. He smiled. The factory was his now.

Alone in the field, Lex suddenly heard something.

'Help me!'

What was it? Then he heard it again.

'Help me!'

He walked through the corn and suddenly there was a scarecrow.

Lex was frightened. *That scarecrow can talk!* he thought. But then it wasn't a scarecrow. It was a teenage boy. The boy was on a big wooden pole. He had no shirt. There was a big red S on the front of his body.

'Help me, please,' he said one more time.

THOOOMMM!!!

The first big meteor crashed into the cornfield. Lex ran.

■ ■ ■

A car stopped opposite Nell's shop on Main Street. Nell took little Lana in her arms and walked out of the shop.

Lewis and Laura Lang were in the car. Lana saw them. 'Mommy! Daddy!' she shouted.

Nell looked up and saw a big meteor in the sky.

THOOOMMM!!!

The meteor crashed into the Langs' car. Lana's parents were dead.

■ ■ ■

Lionel Luthor ran across the cornfield. 'Lex! Where are you?' he shouted.

He saw some red hair on the ground. Then he found his son. Lex was on the ground. He was very frightened. But where was his beautiful red hair? He was nine years old and he now had no hair at all.

■ ■ ■

Jonathan and Martha Kent were on their way home. Suddenly a meteor hit the road behind them.

'What was that, Jonathan?' asked Martha. 'What's happening?'

THOOOMMM!!!

A spaceship crashed into the road in front of them. Jonathan tried to stop the car but it crashed into a cornfield.

When they opened their eyes, they saw a boy. He was about three years old and he had no clothes.

The boy pulled Jonathan's car door. It opened. Then he pulled Martha's car door. It opened too. Martha and Jonathan were very surprised. They were soon out of the car. Martha took the boy in her arms.

'Are you okay?' asked Jonathan.

'Yes, I'm fine. You?' said Martha.

'Yes. Children don't fall from the sky,' Jonathan said.

'Then where did he come from?' Martha asked. 'I don't think his mom and dad are from Kansas!'

'We can't keep him, Martha,' said Jonathan. 'What can we say to people? *"We found him in a cornfield!"*?'

'*We* didn't find *him*, Jonathan,' said Martha. '*He* found *us*.'

CHAPTER 2
Special and different

Jonathan and Martha took the boy home to their farm. They named him Clark. They didn't tell him about his arrival. They didn't tell other people either. If someone asked, they said, 'He's Martha's sister's son. She died.'

They didn't want Clark to be different from other children. But he *was* different. He was special. He was very strong. He was very fast. Nothing hurt him. When he was eight, a big milk can hit his head. It didn't hurt him.

■ ■ ■

2001, Smallville, Kansas, USA.

Clark sat at his computer. Every morning he used the Internet. He wanted to find stories about special people – very strong people, very fast people.

'Clark Kent!' Martha called. 'You're going to be late for the bus!'

'OK, I'm coming,' shouted Clark. He put on his school clothes and shoes, cleaned his room and put his school books in his bag. All in one minute!

Martha came into his room with some clothes.

'You can wear these to the homecoming dance this weekend,' she said.

'I'm not going, Mom,' said Clark. 'I haven't got a girl to go with.'

'Did you ask anyone?' Martha asked.

'No,' he said. He ran down to the kitchen.

'What's that letter, son?' asked Jonathan.

'It's for the football team,' said Clark. 'They want some new players.'

'You can't do it,' said Jonathan.

'Oh, please, Dad,' said Clark. 'I can run slowly. I can be careful.'

'I'm sorry, Clark,' said Jonathan, 'but the answer is no.'

'I don't want to be different,' shouted Clark. 'I can never do normal things. People at school think I'm a loser*.' He ran out of the door.

'We must tell him about the spaceship,' Martha said to Jonathan.

Clark walked to the bus stop. He was late again. The school bus drove off without him.

'Oh, no!' he said. 'Everything's going wrong today.' Suddenly he smiled a big smile.

He turned and ran through the fields at 100 kilometres an hour.

■ ■ ■

The bus arrived at school. Clark's friends, Pete Ross and Chloe Sullivan, were on it. Chloe was new in Smallville. Her dad worked at LuthorCorp. She wrote for the school newspaper and took photos for it. She was always ready with her camera.

*A 'loser' doesn't play sport or have any friends.

'Are you going to the dance with anyone?' Pete asked Chloe.

'No, not yet,' said Chloe.

'Well, if Clark doesn't ask you ...'

'I'm not interested in Clark, Pete,' she said.

'Right,' said Pete. He knew that wasn't true. 'Well, we can go to the dance together if you want,' he said. 'Not boy and girl. Friend and friend.'

Suddenly Clark was there. 'Hi, you two,' he said.

Pete and Chloe were very surprised to see their friend.

'We saw you at your farm,' Chloe said. 'You weren't on the bus!'

'I came a different way,' said Clark.

'Are you ready for the football team, Clark?' asked Pete.

'I'm not going to do it,' said Clark.

'But, Clark,' said Pete, 'do you want to be the scarecrow?'

'The scarecrow!' Chloe said loudly. 'What's the scarecrow?'

'Shh!' said Pete. 'This happens here every year, Chloe. Before the homecoming game, the football players choose someone. A loser. They take him to the cornfield and take all his clothes. Then they write a big red S on the front of his body.'

'And they put him on a big wooden pole,' said Clark. 'So he's a scarecrow.'

'How terrible!' said Chloe.

Then Clark saw a beautiful girl with long, brown hair and a lovely smile.

'See you later,' he said to his friends.

Clark walked across to Lana Lang. He was a metre from her. Suddenly he crashed to the ground. His books went everywhere. *Why does this always happen near Lana?* he thought. *Is it because I like her?*

'Hi, Clark, are you okay?' she asked.

'Hi, Lana,' he said. 'Yeah, I'm fine.'

She gave his books to him.

'You're reading Nietzsche*, huh? Are you man or superman?'

'I don't know,' Clark said.

They smiled.

'Lana!' shouted Whitney Fordman, a tall, good-looking student. He was Lana's boyfriend. Whitney was fantastic at sports. He was in all the school teams.

He ran up and kissed Lana. They walked away together.

* Nietzsche (1844-1900), a German writer and thinker; he wrote about man and superman.

CHAPTER 3
Two terrible shocks

A student looked at the photos of the school sports teams. He looked at the 1989 photo.

'You're late for your class, young man,' said a teacher behind him. The student turned.

'What's your name?' asked the teacher. 'Are you new?'

Suddenly the student hit the teacher in the face. A big blue electric shock went from the student's hand into the teacher's body. The teacher crashed into the wall.

The student took the photo of the three happy football players and left the school.

I'm gonna get you! he thought.

■ ■ ■

Lex Luthor drove his Porsche through the country to the LuthorCorp factory in Smallville.

'The Smallville factory doesn't make any money,' Lionel Luthor said to his son. 'Go to Smallville. Make changes!' So Lex left Metropolis. And here he was. In the centre of nowhere. Great!

Lex arrived at LuthorCorp. He was twenty-one years old and he still had no hair.

He walked into the factory. A man sat at a desk with his lunch.

'Mr Luthor!' the man said, surprised. 'My name's Gabe Sullivan.'

'Call me Lex.'

'The workers aren't happy, Lex,' said Gabe. 'They're frightened about their jobs.'

'It's OK,' said Lex. 'I want everyone to stay.'

'But your father said …'

'I'm not my father,' said Lex Luthor.

Later, Lex drove down a small country road at 100 kilometres an hour. His car radio played loud music.

Not far away, Clark was on a bridge. He looked into the water. He thought about his life and he wasn't happy. He didn't hear Lex Luthor's car.

Lex answered his mobile phone. He didn't look at the road for a minute. He drove onto the bridge. Then he saw Clark. He tried to stop the car but Clark was right in front of him.

I'm going to hit him! Lex thought. Their eyes met. Then Lex's car crashed into Clark.

THOOOMMM!!!

The car and Clark went over the bridge and into the water. Clark's eyes closed and everything went black.

CHAPTER 4
The green necklace

Under the water Clark opened his eyes. He was OK. He wasn't hurt. Then he remembered the car. THE CAR!

He found the car with Lex in it. Lex's eyes were closed. Clark pulled open the door and pulled Lex out. He took him in his arms and started to swim.

When Clark put Lex on the ground, he thought he was dead. Clark put his left hand on Lex's body. Then he put his right hand over his left.

'One, two. One, two. One, two. Come on! Don't die!' he said.

Some water came out of Lex's mouth. He opened his eyes and saw Clark. He was very surprised.

'But I hit you!' he said.

'Well, I'm not dead,' said Clark.

Clark looked at the bridge. *A car hit me at 100 kilometres an hour. I'm not hurt. I am not normal,* he thought.

The police and a doctor arrived. Then Jonathan Kent arrived too.

Jonathan put his arms around Clark. 'Are you OK, son?' he asked.

'I'm fine, Dad,' said Clark.

'I'm Jonathan Kent. This is my son,' Jonathan told a policeman. 'Who was the stupid driver of the car?'

'I was,' said Lex Luthor. 'You have a very special son, Mr Kent,' he said. 'You saved my life, Clark. How can I thank you?'

'Drive more slowly,' said Jonathan.

After dinner that night, Clark went up to his special room in the barn. He looked at the night sky. Then he looked over at the farmhouse next to the Kents' farm.

The front door opened and Lana Lang came out. Clark smiled. But then Whitney came out.

Whitney put his arms around Lana. 'Are you alone tonight?' he asked.

'Yes, Aunt Nell's at Lex Luthor's,' said Lana. 'Did you hear about Clark?' she said. 'He saved Lex's life today.'

'Clark?' Whitney said. 'Clark Kent?'

'Yes,' said Lana. 'Sometimes people can surprise you.'

Whitney didn't want to talk about Clark. He wanted to talk about Whitney.

'I've got a game on Saturday,' he said. 'Some important people are going to be there.'

'That's great!' Lana said. Whitney wanted to be a top football player. It was his dream.

She gave her green necklace to him. The necklace was part of a meteor. A special meteor. This meteor hit Lana's parents' car.

'I can't take this, Lana,' Whitney said. 'It means everything to you.'

'Keep it just for the game,' she said. He put it in his jacket. Then he kissed her.

CHAPTER 5
The true story

Tony Carozza had a job at a car place. It was evening. It was almost time to go home.

A boy came into the shop.

'I'm sorry,' said Tony. 'We're closed.'

The boy said nothing. Tony looked at him carefully.

'I know you,' he said. 'You were that scarecrow years ago! What happened to you? Why aren't you older?'

The boy still said nothing.

'Answer me, Stupid!' said Tony. 'I'm talking to you!'

The boy suddenly hit Tony in the face. A big blue electric shock went from his hand into Tony Carozza's body. Tony crashed onto the floor. He didn't move. On the wall, there was a photo of three happy football players.

The boy smiled and left the shop.

■ ■ ■

It was the day after the car crash. When Clark walked into school, every student said, 'Nice work, Clark!'

'Am I at the right school?' Clark asked Pete and Chloe.

'You saved Lex Luthor's life,' said Chloe. 'This is going in the school newspaper.'

'My dad hates the Luthors,' said Pete.

'Yes, but *Lionel* Luthor bought your dad's factory. Not *Lex*,' said Clark.

When Clark arrived home on the farm that afternoon, he found a new red car in front of the house. There was a letter on the car. Clark opened it.

Thank you, Clark, he read. *I hope you like red.*

Clark looked at the car. He was very excited.

'You can't keep it, Clark,' Jonathan said.

'Why not?'

'Because the Luthors aren't good people. They're rich thanks to Smallville. They bought our friends' houses and their farms.'

'Lex's father did all that,' said Clark. 'Not Lex.'

'I'm sorry, Clark,' Jonathan said. 'I know you're angry.'

'Angry!' shouted Clark. 'You have no idea!' He ran up to his room in the barn.

'You must tell him now,' Martha said.

Jonathan went to Clark's room. He put his arms around his son. 'I'm going to tell you the story of the day of the meteors,' he said.

He gave Clark a picture. There were lots of letters and numbers on it. Was it a language?

'I think this is from your mom and dad,' he said.

'What does it say?' Clark asked.

'I have no idea,' said Jonathan. 'They came from a different world.'

'A different world?!' laughed Clark. 'So I arrived in a spaceship? That's stupid!'

'Do you want to see that spaceship?' asked Jonathan. 'It's under the barn.'

When he saw the little spaceship, Clark was very angry.

'Why didn't you tell me this before?' he shouted. He ran out of the barn.

CHAPTER 6
A quick kiss

Lana Lang looked at the words: *Lewis Lang 1957-1989 Laura Lang 1959-1989*. She heard something behind her.

'Who's there?' she called.

'It's me. It's Clark,' he said. 'What are *you* doing here?'

Lana looked at Clark. He was nice.

'Please don't tell anyone,' she said. 'I come here to talk to my mom and dad. Is that stupid?'

'No, it isn't stupid,' Clark said. 'Do you remember them?'

'Not very well,' said Lana. 'They died when I was three. Do you want to meet them?'

She sat on the ground. 'Mom, Dad, this is Clark Kent,' she said.

'Hi, Mr and Mrs Lang,' said Clark. 'I'm sorry? What's that?' He sat down and listened.

'Your mom says, "You're never alone, Lana,"' he said, 'and your dad says, "You're beautiful."'

Lana smiled. 'Thank you, Clark,' she said.

'Can I walk home with you?' asked Clark.

'Yes. Thanks,' said Lana.

When they arrived at Lana's house, she said, 'We talked for a long time tonight, Clark. It was nice.' She kissed him quickly. 'Good night, Clark.' She ran into the house.

Clark was very happy. But there was someone at Lana's house. He saw the kiss and he was very angry. It was Whitney Fordman.

The next day before school, Clark drove the red car back to Lex Luthor's house. The house was big and old. The front door was open. Clark walked in.

'Hello!' he shouted. 'Is anyone at home?'

'Clark,' said Lex. 'What are you doing here? How's your new car?'

'I love it,' said Clark. 'But I can't keep it.'

'Why not? You saved my life, Clark. I want to thank you,' Lex said. Then he said, 'Oh, I get it. Your dad doesn't like me.'

Clark didn't say anything.

'It's OK,' said Lex, 'I understand.'

'It's not you,' said Clark. 'He doesn't like your father. Thank you for the car, Lex. I'm sorry I can't keep it.'

'I changed after that crash,' said Lex. 'When I was under the water … I saw my life in Smallville in a new way. I can see now … this isn't the end of my old life in Metropolis … it's the start of my new life here. So, thank you, Clark. I hope we can be friends for a long time.'

CHAPTER 7
This year's scarecrow

When school finished that afternoon, Chloe and Pete went into town. There were people and police cars in front of one of the shops. And a man was on the ground.

'What happened here?' asked Chloe.

'It's Freddie Post. He had a big electric shock,' said a man.

Chloe turned to Pete. 'He's the third one this week,' she said. 'And here's something interesting. They were all in the school football team in 1989.'

Pete looked at the people by the body. He saw a teenage boy. 'Who's that boy?' he asked.

'I don't know,' said Chloe. She quickly took a photo of him.

The two friends walked back to the school and went to the newspaper room.

'I'm going to put this photo into the computer,' she said. 'Can you find the 1989 yearbook*, Pete?'

A few minutes later Pete sat next to Chloe with the book. 'Chloe, look!' he said. 'This boy, twelve years ago. His name's Jeremy Creek.'

Chloe looked at the book and then at her photo. 'It's the same person,' she said. 'And he's the same age. That's interesting!'

Chloe and Pete used the Internet and wrote emails. They found old newspapers.

'I'm going to find Clark,' said Pete. 'We must tell him about this.'

Pete came back with Clark.

Clark looked at the two photos of Jeremy Creek.

* A school yearbook has photos of all the students in their last year at that school.

'Jeremy had a big electric shock twelve years ago,' said Chloe. 'He was in hospital for twelve years. A few days ago he woke up and ran away.'

'So why is he back in Smallville?' asked Clark. 'Why is he giving electric shocks to people?'

'Because twelve years ago,' Pete said, 'they put him on a pole in a field. He was that year's scarecrow!'

'The meteors crashed into Smallville that day!' said Chloe.

Oh no! thought Clark. *All this happened because of me! That was the day of my arrival.*

He looked at a photo in one of the old newspapers. It was a little girl. She had a terrible look on her face. It said under the photo, *Meteor hits mom and dad*.

'So what do you think, Clark?' asked Chloe.

Clark knew that little face in the photo. 'Oh no! Lana!'

'Why didn't you tell me about this before?' he shouted. 'I did this!'

He ran from the room.

■ ■ ■

In front of the school he met Whitney.

'Hi, Clark,' said Whitney. 'I'm looking for you. You're this year's scarecrow!'

'Leave me alone, Whitney,' said Clark angrily, 'or I'm going to ...'

'You're going to what?' said Whitney. 'Come on, Clark. Hit me!' He took off his jacket.

Clark moved nearer to Whitney but he suddenly started to fall. He saw Lana's green necklace under Whitney's open T-shirt.

'What's between you and Lana?' shouted Whitney. 'You can have her necklace!' He took off the necklace and put it on Clark. 'But you can't have Lana! *I'm* taking her to the dance tonight.'

Clark didn't feel well. He tried to move. And then everything went black. Whitney and two of his friends put him in a car.

Jeremy Creek watched everything. And he remembered this day, twelve years ago.

CHAPTER 8
A big red S

Clark woke up. He was in a cornfield, on a pole. He was very cold. It was night and it was October. He looked down. There was a big red S on the front of his body.

He tried to move his arms. *I can't move. What's wrong with me?* he thought. *It's the necklace!*

Suddenly there was a boy in front of him. 'It hurts,' said the boy. 'I remember that.'

'You're Jeremy Creek,' said Clark.

'No. Jeremy Creek died twelve years ago,' said the boy. He started to walk away.

'Where are you going?' asked Clark.

'To the school dance,' said Jeremy. 'I didn't go in 1989.'

'Please help me,' said Clark.

'No,' Jeremy said. 'You stay here. I don't want to hurt you.'

■ ■ ■

Jeremy walked down the road. Lex Luthor drove by and saw him.

'I know that boy,' he thought. 'But how? From where?'

He stopped the car. Then he remembered the field twelve years ago. The boy on the pole. The big red S. He got out of the car and went into the field.

'Help me,' he heard. 'Help me, please.'

It's not possible, Lex thought.

Then he saw him. 'Clark!' he shouted.

Lex helped Clark. Clark pulled off the necklace.

'You need a doctor, Clark,' Lex said.

Without the necklace, Clark was suddenly Clark again. He didn't need a doctor.

'I'm OK. Thanks, Lex,' he said. He found his clothes and ran into the night. Lex saw the necklace on the ground. He put it in his jacket and walked back to his car.

■ ■ ■

At the school dance, the band played and everyone danced.

Jeremy Creek didn't dance. He was behind the school building. He opened the door of a large box. *WATER,* it said.

They're all going to die now, he thought.

Suddenly Clark was behind him.

'Stop this now, Jeremy,' he said.

'You!' said Jeremy. 'What are you doing here?'

'You're not going to hurt my friends,' said Clark.

'You don't understand,' said Jeremy. 'I'm doing this for you and the others. No more scarecrows!'

'No, Jeremy. Stop it,' said Clark.

Jeremy hit Clark in the face but he had a surprise. Clark wasn't hurt.

There was a car next to Jeremy. He opened the door and started it. He drove at Clark. Clark put his arms in front of him, but Jeremy didn't stop. Clark was on the front of the car when it hit the Water box. There was water everywhere. It gave Jeremy a big electric shock. His body was blue. Then everything was quiet.

Clark pulled the car door. It opened. 'Are you OK?' he asked.

'Who are you?' asked Jeremy. 'I want to go home.'

■ ■ ■

Clark watched the end of the homecoming dance. Lana and Whitney danced in the centre of the room. Then they kissed. A long kiss. Clark was sad. He turned and left.

There were three cars in a line in the car park. *That's Whitney's car and his friends' cars,* Clark thought. He had an idea.

He took one car and put it on top of another one. Then he took the third car and put it on top of the other two. He waited.

When students came out and saw the cars, they laughed.

Then Whitney came out, with his arm around Lana. He saw his car.

'Who did this to my car?' he shouted angrily. Everyone laughed and Lana smiled.

EPILOGUE
'Thanks for the dance'

'Clark,' called Jonathan when he came home. 'Lex was here. This is for you.' He gave Clark a small box and a letter. Lana's necklace was in the box. Clark read the letter.

I found this necklace in the cornfield, Clark. We are friends now, so please keep this box. My mother gave it to me many years ago. It's very special. Lex.

Clark opened the box and saw the necklace. He didn't feel well. He closed the box again, and he was OK. It *was* a special box.

'I must remember that,' he thought.

■ ■ ■

'Hello, Clark.' It was Lana. In his room in the barn.

'Lana!' he said, surprised. 'What are you doing here?'

'You didn't come to the dance,' she said. She walked up to him and put her arms around him.

'Let's dance now.'

They danced to the music. Clark closed his eyes. Suddenly he heard a car. He opened his eyes. Lana wasn't there. It was a daydream.

■ ■ ■

He looked through the window. A car arrived at Lana's house.

'The necklace!' Clark took it to Lana's house. He put it on her front door. He was back in his room before Lana opened the car door. He moved faster than the wind and nobody saw him.

When Lana arrived at her front door, she saw the necklace. She took it and put it on. *Oh Whitney, you are fantastic,* she thought.

'Good night, Lana,' Clark said quietly. 'Thanks for the dance.'

SMALLVILLE on TV

***Smallville* was first on TV in 2001. Teenagers all over the world loved it. It is the story of Clark Kent before he became Superman.**

The pilot: *Arrival*

Arrival was the first ever *Smallville* programme. It was the pilot. A pilot TV programme is a test programme. Sometimes people like the pilot and they make a series. Sometimes people don't like the pilot and they don't make the series. The programme makers had a lot of work to do for the pilot.

The story

Miles Millar and Alfred Gough worked on the *Smallville* story from the start. It tells the story of Clark's arrival from space and his life as a teenager. 'We wanted to go into Clark's head,' said Millar. 'Who is he?' they wanted to know.

Most of the *Smallville* characters come from Superman comics. Chloe Sullivan was a new character. 'Chloe comes from Metropolis,' said Millar. 'She sees things differently from Smallville people. She's always asking questions.'

The place

Smallville is a small, quiet, all-American town. 'We looked for "Smalltown, USA",' said Gough. 'We wanted a nice, clean town.' First, they thought about Australia. In the end, they filmed in Vancouver in Canada.

The actors

The *Smallville* team found the *Smallville* actors for the pilot in five months. They looked all over America and Canada.

First, they found Lana (Kristin Kreuk). They loved her. 'She's the one,' they said. Then they found Clark (Tom Welling). Kristin and

What do these words mean? You can use a dictionary.
actor to become character programme series

Find out more about *Smallville* at www.KryptonSite.com

Tom were good together on TV.

'People must like the *Smallville* characters,' Gough said. 'They're coming into their living rooms every week.'

The character of Pete was a problem for the team. No one was right. They looked for months. At last, they saw Sam Jones III and they liked him. That was lucky because they started to film four days later!

After the pilot

The *Smallville* team filmed *Arrival* in 16 days. Then, they waited. Over eight million people watched *Smallville: Arrival*. It was a big hit. 'Clark Kent can fly, and this programme's going to fly,' said one newspaper.

Now, *Smallville* is in its fifth series. There are *Smallville* books and CDs. *Smallville* is here to stay!

Do you watch *Smallville* on TV?
Who's your favourite *Smallville* character? Why?

SMALLVILLE™
the people

Smallville isn't just a programme about other planets and people with strange powers. It's also about teenagers and their problems. They are all trying to be normal in a very strange town!

"Sometimes people can surprise you."

CLARK KENT

Clark just wants to be a normal teenager. He wants to play football and go to the school dance. Why is Clark so unhappy?

Clark's big secret

He can run very fast and he is very strong. Nothing can hurt him. But Clark can't tell anyone these things. He can't tell his closest friends, Chloe and Pete. He feels alone.

"I don't want to be different. I can never do normal things. People at school think I'm a loser."

LANA LANG

Lana Lang – the homecoming queen. She's beautiful and she has lots of friends. Her boyfriend, Whitney, loves her, but she feels alone too.

Clark and Lana

Clark is always dreaming about Lana. He loves her but he can't be near her. She wears a bit of the meteor as a necklace – it's a bit of kryptonite. Clark comes from the planet Krypton. Clark can't use his powers when he's near kryptonite. But in this story, Clark doesn't know that!

In *Arrival* Clark and Lana become friends. Lana knows that Clark is special. Later in the series, Lana and Clark become boyfriend and girlfriend.

LEX LUTHOR

Lex is rich but he isn't always happy. His father, Lionel Luthor, doesn't love him. His mother and brother are dead. A lot of people in Smallville hate the Luthor family. But Lex is different from his father.

In *Arrival*, Lex and Clark meet for the first time. Lex wants to know more about Clark Kent. Who is he? How did he save his life? Lex wants some answers. He decides to stay in Smallville.

Lex and Clark become friends. But there is a dark Lex. We first meet him in Series 4 of *Smallville*. Black kryptonite breaks Lex in two. The dark Lex, called Alexander, appears.

CHLOE AND PETE

Chloe, Pete and Clark are good friends. They feel different from the other students. But it's not always easy to be friends. Pete likes Chloe, but Chloe likes Clark. And Clark loves Lana!

Why is Clark special to Lana, do you think? Who will be stronger – the good Lex or the dark Lex? Talk to other students.

What do these words mean? You can use a dictionary.

to become planet powers secret strange

Lex Luthor with his father, Lionel

"I don't want to be my father."

"Now here's something interesting…"

Hom

What is homecoming?

It's an exciting time for high school students in America. Old students come home and visit their old school or town.

How did it start?

It started in the late 1800s. People often left their hometowns because there weren't any jobs. Once a year, they came home for a party. Now homecoming week usually happens at the town high school in late September or October.

What happens in homecoming week?

There is usually a big football game against a school from a different town. There is also a parade through the town with the high school band. For the school students there are 'dress-up' days. Students wear fun clothes. And on the Friday of homecoming week, students wear their school colours. The week ends with the homecoming dance.

Who are the homecoming king and queen?

The homecoming king and queen are the stars of homecoming week! They are in their last year of high school. They usually have lots of friends and are very good-looking. The other students choose them. In *Arrival*, Whitney and Lana are the homecoming king and queen.

What do you think of homecoming week?
What happens at schools in your country at the end of the year?

ecoming

A homecoming queen and her friends

What is the homecoming dance?

The homecoming dance is often in the high school building. There is a DJ or a band. The students wear their best clothes. A lot of students go to the dance with a date. In *Arrival*, Clark is sad because he doesn't have a date for the dance. The homecoming king and queen have one slow dance together.

Is it always fun?

Homecoming week isn't fun for everyone. Some high schools don't have it because it can bring problems. Some students feel alone because they don't have a date for the homecoming dance. And sometimes students do stupid things. Whitney and his friends put Clark on the wooden pole in *Arrival*.

Does it happen in the UK?

No, British schools don't have a homecoming week. Before students leave school, there is often a leavers' dance. Everyone dresses up.

What do these words mean? You can use a dictionary.

date king parade queen to dress up

CHAPTERS 1–2

Before you read

You can use your dictionary for these questions.

1 Do you find these on a farm or in the sky?

scarecrow **cornfield** **helicopter**
meteor **barn** **spaceship** **wooden pole**

2 Look at People and Places on pages 4 and 5. Find the mistakes in these sentences.

a) Clark Kent is from Smallville.
b) There are a lot of factories in Smallville.
c) Lana loves Clark.
d) Pete is from Metropolis.
e) Whitney is great at sports and a great person.

3 Do you like the city or the country? Talk to other students.

After you read

4 Who is it?

a) Her parents die when she is three.
b) They want a child very much.
c) He doesn't want to be different. He wants to be normal.
d) He is tall, good-looking and very good at sport.
e) She writes for the school newspaper and likes taking photos.

5 Answer the questions.

a) The title of the book is *Arrival*.
Who arrives? *How* does he arrive? *When* and *where* does he arrive? *Who* does he find?
b) Why doesn't Lex Luthor have any hair?
c) In what ways is Clark special?
d) Why can't Clark play for the football team?
e) What's the 'scarecrow'?

6 What do you think?

a) Why does Clark always crash to the ground when he's near Lana?
b) Who is going to be Lana's boyfriend at the end? Clark or Whitney?

CHAPTERS 3–6

Before you read

7 Find the right word. You can use your dictionary.

bridge **electric shock** **necklace**

a) You can die from this.
b) You can walk across water or a road on this.
c) You can wear this.

After you read

8 Use these words to complete the sentences. Put them in the past tense.

arrive **crash** **hit** **hurt** **kiss** **meet** **save**

a) The student __________ the teacher in the face.
b) Lex __________ at LutherCorp in his car.
c) He went into the factory and __________ Gabe Sullivan.
d) Lex's car __________ into Clark but it (not) __________ him. Clark was OK.
e) Clark __________ Lex Luthor's life.
f) Lana __________ Clark and ran into the house.

9 Are these sentences right or wrong?

a) The student took a photo of four sad basketball players and left the school.
b) Lex crashed because he answered his mobile phone.
c) Lana's green necklace was part of a meteor. She gave it to Whitney.
d) Lex gave Clark a new red car to say 'thank you'.
e) When Jonathan told Clark about his arrival in Smallville, Clark was very happy.
f) Clark had the red car for many years.

10 What do you think?

a) On page 14 a student says, 'I'm gonna get you!' Who is he?
b) Why is the green necklace important?
c) Why does the boy give Tony Carozza an electric shock?
d) How does Whitney feel when he sees Lana kiss Clark? What is he going to do?

CHAPTERS 7–Epilogue

Before you read

11 What is going to happen?

a) Who is going to be 'this year's scarecrow' and have 'a big red S'?

b) Who is going to dance with Lana at the homecoming dance?

After you read

12 Look at your answers to Exercise 11. Were you right?

13 Answer the questions.

a) What does Clark suddenly learn about Lana?

b) How does Clark feel when he's near the necklace?

c) Who doesn't help Clark?

d) Who helps him?

e) What happens to Jeremy at the school dance?

f) What does Clark do to Whitney's car?

g) What does Lex give Clark? Why is it 'very special'?

h) Does Clark dance with Lana at the end of the story?

14 You are Jeremy Creek. What happened to you? Tell your story.

15 You are Chloe. Write about the homecoming dance for the school newspaper.

16 What do you think?

a) Do you like the end of the story?

b) Can you think of a different end?